# LAST OF THE COALMINE CHOIRBOYS

## GRAEME RICHARDSON

**NEW WALK EDITIONS**
**Nottingham & Leicester**

978-1-7392812-5-0

Published by New Walk Editions
c/o Rory Waterman, Department of Humanities,
Hollymount House, Nottingham Trent University, NG1 4FQ
and
c/o Nick Everett, Centre for New Writing,
Attenborough Tower, University of Leicester, LE1 7RH

www.newwalkmagazine.com

Printed by imprintdigital, Upton Pyne, Exeter.

# Contents

# Pithead

Lady – bear with me now –
here's an old miner's tale of woe
that somehow, through the years
of continual warring grimness,
my absent-minded lies
and empty-headed idiocies,
I've not forgotten.
Those stories had the same aim.
Practical jokes, horseplay in the shower –
the most important part of all that gear
was the coping mechanism.
That, and the snap-tin.
Snap left out, you're asking for it,
pit-ponies would snaffle it,
fond of a jam sandwich, snatch it
even from the pocket of your jacket.
And this, I used to love hearing:
a tired and barkled collier returned
to his coat once and found
a pony had had his bloody orange.
You'd think it was safe in your duds.
But the bugger snuck his muzzle in,
such tender cunning, nuzzling
flesh and juice through the threads.
Buried life. Plodding the tunnels,
pulling tubs in skull-cap and bridle.
Who would deny him that sunburst dazzle –
all sweetness, and breezy fields?

## Bearings

One poor dear – 84, in the hospice,
just a few picked chicken-bones
under the sheets, fists
bulbs of dried garlic,
and a head of dandelion fluff
almost blown –
before she finally gave up
cried out all night for her Mum.

Sometimes my kids cry out for me.
Easier to get out of bed, though,
than to get out of sleep.
I can't get my bearings.
Where can they be?
Where has the door gone?

# Unlatched and Lit

*for the choirs of St Peter and St Paul's, Mansfield,*
*and St Peter's, Harborne*

This sanctuary of my soul
at midnight is a seam of coal,
packed with power but hard to break.
I mine it as I lie awake.

Pixellated, hassock-wool
Angel, Lion, Eagle, Bull;
cobweb-fur in every lock,
stained-glass windows' dull mock-croc,

crossed keys, swords, reclining stags,
on the rafters' tattered flags
gossamer as candle-smoke
gathered under Sherwood oak.

On deep sills, in each chipped vase,
Oasis stinks beneath the flowers,
countered by the vestry's whiff
of Brasso, beeswax, Vim and Jif.

All those stories – well-known, once,
lost sheep, lost coin, and then lost sons –
whisper to a heavenly host
of woodworm, rats, and plaintive ghosts.

Here, before these well-worn pews,
children walked in polished shoes
unsteadily processing in
and never coming out again.

# Mansfield Notts

Stand outside the old sandstone school – St. John's. Look around
at the battling terraced houses: square, solid, squat.
The road that snarls to the doorsteps, and the windows boarded-up,
and the furious scribble of briar, crossing out a derelict lot.

When I was there, the mines made a brave attempt at colour and pride:
galas, banners, marching bands – even a majorette.
All talk was Thatcher and Scargill, but the Dukeries wouldn't strike
for a future they didn't believe in, and a past they'd best forget.

The earth being almost exhausted, they built in another direction:
pallets, skips, and scrap-yards; superstores, car-parks, flats;
the library with its lift, and a café on the top-floor,
and the blackberry bushes stretching up on the spoil-tip ziggurats.

Children stayed at the surface – and these were their surfaces:
lacquered plywood, linoleum; the varnish of wheel-back chairs;
amber tiles, in butterscotch bathrooms, embossed with sheaves of wheat;
tortoise-shell scabs on jam-tart wounds from the burn of carpeted stairs.

I learnt about success. Success was surviving pain:
stabbing between our fingers with a compass-spike in maths.
Tears were always denied, the earliest self-betrayal,
blamed on cigarettes, or the chlorine of the public baths.

I looked at pain in Leeming Street and on the Bull Farm estate,
and by the Metal Box factory, and the gates of Thompson's grave;
in the bus-station's grimy concrete, or the subway's percussive tunnel;
out to King's Mill Hospital, and back to the Rock Hill caves.

The church was wholly different; the lychgate stopping cars,
and no commercial point to the narrow, impossible steeple,
or the carvings no-one could see, high in the walls and the roof,
and the green where no-one played, with its hillocks of sleeping people.

It was a mine of pain, in its sorrowing, sighing words
painful for martyrs to understand, or empires to misconstrue;
and its hero, the bloodied man descended into hell
who came up again good as new.

# Those Amiable Dwellings

Not for the last time, I needed my sight corrected.
Dettol-sting tears in cushioned corridors,
humbled by the hospital's backless patterned gown.
Doctors on their rounds gave nurses instructions:
Touch and go, touch and go.

First time on my own. I took flight to my dug-outs and bunkers:
Harlow Wood dell of yellow-flowered gorse, or
those snug enclosed hollows, the den
in the hillside's rogue rhododendron, escaped
from a local stately home.

That landscape, butchered and gouged by industry –
Ratcher Hill Quarry, Ling Forest, Thieves Wood –
a glittering reservoir, for those who know the trick,
who going through the vale of misery use it for a well
and the pools are full of water.

I tried to remember whole psalms and descants.
The weekend way to Strawberry Knob:
hawthorn and heather. Ash-grey soil.
The golden oak-leaves got the light, and the darkness
comprehended it not.

Coke-furnace sunset in Clipstone Forest.
The headstocks grazing peacefully in the distance.
Before the sponsored walk, Dad would drive us round,
marking out the route with sawdust arrows,
Sports Report on the radio.

I cried for my mum, but was told that wouldn't do.
I tried a low whistle of 'Brother James's Air'.
I thought of our arrows marking the track,
starting off clumsy, peaking in the middle, then
tailing off, becoming slapdash.

I woke, and wore an eye-patch for a week.
Elastoplast-pink, though. Hardly piratical.
I remembered acutely the torments of the ward,
and knew it was one of those things you never
speak of but store securely away.

When I stand on the edge of another black pit,
I make the same journey, give the same recital.
The choir's no more. The hospital bulldozed.
The dell replaced by quality housing. Gorse and heather
pulled up with the roots.

But the dove came back at least once to the ark
with nothing, before that triumphant olive-leaf.
So, in the dwindling forest, I sift out sawdust from my fist:
grain that unless it falls to the ground and dies
remains alone.

# Dust-Bunnies in the Playboy Mansion

God, the perils of the flesh were tiring. At the peak of my mania I found it therapeutic to hoover the cathedral. Not a euphemism. It had to be done in the morning, before the arrival of gockles and gawpers. Already it was hot but that building was a cavernous fridge. The machine I dragged along was the last of its kind, a clanking metal pachyderm on wheels. As it trundled, roaring, over the Norman slabs, I struggled to control the enormous throbbing nozzle. Put your back into it, the Verger would chuckle, you're doing God's work.

Hark how the heavenly anthem drowns all music but its own. Dust and loose threads mustered in corners, cute furry creatures I half-expected to scurry away before my probing. I sucked them up with glee. Spiders in their rigging fought back in the hurricane, but they too eventually succumbed. Shed skin and Sunday-best lint formed little drifts on the chancel steps. There must be enough DNA here, I thought, to conjure up Frankenstein's Congregant and lead him to the font. Maybe one day he could take over the hoovering.

Tick tock in heels, a lady came to say an encouraging word. I saw the small damp hairs at her neck. 'I should be out in the garden in my bikini' she said. Oh Christ. Just then, a buzz, a flapping sound. A coin? A scattered pearl? Or just a bearded jelly-baby? I groped for that red button, the size of a macaroon. But with the vacuum cleaner off, the sound continued. I stepped back and peered at the heavens.

Up by a clerestory window, a trapped blackbird hovered. An expert in praise, for whom every black hole can become a singing wine-glass, in sunlight ascending and descending, beyond all reason, born for this from the breakthrough of hatching, fluttering at that glory, a desperate tongue.

Nothing doing, I turned the machine back on. Show them what you're made of son.

# Fauré

Column capitals, buttered-up in smears
from the west window; gaping golden chairs;
the fervent choir, stacked, with five bulging flats
to milk, swayed in the slippery triplets.

So what if it seemed a bit routine –
tucking her hair back and taking me in?
Cockily, blinded, I sang, embracing
the mood of the cunt-eager Jean Racine,

soft-soaping that sun-king-lookalike God.
The throb and fall of each unctuous chord
left me light-headed. I glanced at her, down
among the altos, forming with a scowl

and a headshake each French word, as one whose
conscience is musical and these are lies.
Angels, sunlight, throw yourselves over her –
*que tout l'enfer fuie au son de ta voix…*

I haven't heard it since all hell broke loose,
when I learnt to tell what was lip-service,
when clichés stopped coming *cantabile*,
when all that *legato* flow turned to bile.

# Desertification

It was hard, under the hose-pipe ban. A peach of a world became a pumice stone. The dog's rough tongue a dead man lolling into town still saddled on his wild-eyed horse. The stream had thrown its shining rider and went bareback, stinking, lost. Through the fields, sandpaper paths. Friction-burns were rife in the park for pink-hot kids, diving and skidding. Goal-posts were t-shirts, fought off like vultures, or bikes, stricken beasts picked clean.

Though also my bones, in their moist cladding, creaked and stiffened under the skin, my whole body sobbed with perspiration, the lawn only lush round my lounger: I was a juicy oasis in myself! Eating nothing all day but salt-gritty crisps, I could still piss for England – even on nights of Bulgarian cornershop-red pushing its lively-pulsed arm up my throat, a drowning boy grabbing at weeds.

Hay-fever flow steamed off in the sun, its clouds to water more pollen-full grasses. Over my damp sheets epic snail-trails, and the opposite of tears. I rang her most days. She was, her sister said, invariably, in the bath.

## C90s

Slyly, idly, I look for you online;
sleepless, tossed from my own bed by a scream.
But you elude enlargements of the screen
(could that be you? Fatter now, saturnine,
grimacing under a strange married name?)
and shame needs no updates. Picture the scene:

every cloud had flowered into cornflower blue
over the meadow's old lace, late snow.
Water ran off clear. April would be warm.
I got this from a book, but was it true?
(Except by saying it, how could I know?)
*I am at rest with you, I have come home.*

What were you like then? Never alone.
Your youngish mother gave you older tastes
in clothes, music, men… You had her mix-tapes,
marked in fading biro, off-white as bone –
they soothed you, a baby, full-lipped, round-faced,
surprised by your own mess, your own mistakes.

I threw them out, your reliquary songs:
cassettes of white-appropriated blues
whose bobbins, turning, turned each other on
until one stalled, and, so far strung along,
the other sent disconsolate lassoes
that crumpled up, all magnetism down,

no rest, nor home, not now. At 4am –
pop-ups of sites too toxic to visit,
the browser's freeze a feature not a glitch,
memory full – there you are, here I am.
One beggar's moment out of the blizzard.
That wide blue sky. Those paths. That crystal ditch.

## To the Quick

Drank a quart of whisky neat.
Hoped to drop. Stayed on my feet.

Used the mirror by my bed
every morning: still not dead.

Talked at friends, hour after hour,
calmly logical, if sour.

Felt no damage, felt no pain,
however loudly I'd complain.

But time is sharp: only that
cut from the heart its veil of fat.

# Lemon Pip

Nestled in acid,
in fine bitter spray,
in a wincing air-kiss
you are spat out,
spurt from plucking,
niggle at hangnails,
hamper and devil
cocktails and cakes.
Sharp as a fish-bone,
broad-bean-waxy,
elusive as a name
or the earliest dream,
you huddle around
the squeezer's dome,
grey-green, wizened;
as if you once lived
pink and hearty
and cradled:
a zestling.

## After the Death of a Child (A Pastoral Heckle)

The dead live on in memory? Not true.
They lodge there dead, and yours not theirs the hell.
The world without them waits, besieging you;
their corpse within you, poisoning the well.
That body was, by all your senses, known,
with knowledge more acute now 'it' is ash.
The rescuer, sent out, returns alone,
and relic-hunters come to you with trash,
and every consolation seems a lie:
no 'letting be', no 'love in letting go',
no 'harvest' in a void; the sun has gone
to pieces in the song-forsaken sky
and night withdraws the way, and you don't know
how – *thank you, yes, it's ten years* – you live on.

# Baby Steps

You come forward, awed at finding your feet;
    queasily totter; then flail on one leg,
Chaplin cornering. The light breeze floors you,
    a horseshoe in its glove. You glare, get up,
as easily led as rising water
    and, with limp tattered twigs and tiny rocks
in tight fistfuls, just as acquisitive.
    I watch. I almost blister as I wait.

You were the one we, spitting each midnight,
    moneyless, thought we would be forced to scotch.
You heard as whales hear a ship overturn,
    and persist in their deeps, and past them spears
and hooks dwindle, newly blind and inert.
    Now swallow the man of calamity
in that gummy all-wowing smile, drown his
    spine-song (*love and da-mage, love and da-mage*).

I learnt about children from their mourners;
    in canteens where sugary tea congeals
while everyone tries to get their breath back
    and never will; or, in the viewing-room,
dim, net-curtained, peering over the edge
    of a small white box that's somehow also
a volcano unhinging its jaw; once
    blocking off the 'wrong' side, powdered black cracks

in the fixed young face; their faces crumple
    and fold like old pumpkins. Who willingly
would give their body to this quicklime hold?
    We could end up left behind. Your hand lifts
open, a crown splash of rain, offering
    one strawberry-snail shell, and one acorn,
split and sprouting in the fall: effigy
    and crude prototype. Not choices but gifts.

# Aubade

Lost winning ticket found new every morning –
you say *don't squeeze too tight* but I gloat
over you – I exult, a dog beyond grabbing,
under a hedge, with the stolen Sunday roast;
I'm jubilant, that one desperate duck
who chainsaws through the crowd and swipes
the last piece of crust, and just as heedless
of the rest, the crestfallen, the starving standing by –
you are mine.

Too late I remember this is rush-hour –
where the pigeons start, and with them all
the piffling tasks of the week – a record-scratch take-off,
a falling-books flutter, the head-in-hands 'Noooooo'
of spillage or breakage – every pause too short,
every ledge a rebuke of pins and goads…
Now, my pretty, we are at the school,
and this is by the crossing,
waiting for the light that says you can go.

# Toys

Hunter of shipwrecks, I follow the debris trail;
kidnapper-quick, I chloroform the talking doll;
battlefield-ghoul, I tiptoe between the remains:
the Lego-shrapnel, the fallen Barbies and Kens.

Weariness, from the soles of the feet to the scalp.
Usual remedies, coffee or wine, don't help
with no problem being either woken or numb.
Just give me my orders in frantic, angry mime.

For fun, I imagine the scene when I'm knackered
for good: lying with gathered fragments by my bed,
at one with playthings long lost or loved to bits then.
Ah, the self-*fucking*-pity – my adrenalin!

Your 'borrowed' bouquets of roses billow like dust.
What if, Sweet Avalanche, this, in the end, sufficed?
Time's own rhythm of slip and grip, and in its sweep
all the charmed detritus it picks up.  It picks up.

# Viaduct

Under the railway bridge, I think of jumping.
   Becoming,
      at that
         question-
      mark's
     low-
     point
     a

     dot.
Whip-zoom close-up head-shot of falling.
Result? Not exactly flattering.

Born in a mess, we die in a mess,
on a care-home's plastic cushions,
or a hospital's swiss-army bed,
peaks and troughs of our life a puddle –
why not flatten them here? Run over by
gravity, a truck full of grown-old grudges.

Someone has built a mini shrine.
Washed-out toys and pallid trinkets.
A line of plants. A little fence
that keeps no scavengers out.
Lugworm heaps of bird-shit.
A dagger-cross sunk deep.

You two wait, grinning on your bikes.
We look up to the vaulting bricks.
Hello, you shout – hell-low, hell-low.

Yours are the only answers.

# One More Last Word from the Cross

*i.m. Matt Carver*

Cream in the coffee tumbles and writhes;
exhaust-pipes in the road-side's
blackened gravel twist and turn;
the river's gut-feelings of fear and revulsion
send it running from the town,
as I run from you.

Smokers in drizzle dip a toe in the water;
with cortisone injections, England's
hope of glory, out in the middle,
battles on; westward bound,
roads and their roadkill lie open:
I open to you.

Dead-weight tonnage, the church towers
over the town, a great cloud.
I park under chestnut trees.
His family at the lych-gate
standing, they couldn't say how.
And I stand for you.

Keening, those chestnuts lurch and sway;
bowling through the pain
the river gently guides him home;
we enter the cloud and stand in its smoke
as it tumbles and writhes.
You say:

*I am the Resurrection and the Life.*

# Last of the Coalmine Choirboys

With Evensong we buried him,
    The quick who loved the dead;
With ruff starched tight, and surplice white,
    And cassock royal red.

Responses were by Gibbons.
    The psalm-chant was by Smart.
Tchaikovsky's Hymn of the Cherubim
    Followed 'As Pants The Hart'.

The echoes prized each beautifully
    Articulated word;
The diction crisp, no slur or lisp,
    Through canticles by Byrd.

But turn to the heavy Bible,
    Caress the ribbon down;
Though edged with gold, it's coarse and old,
    The corners torn and brown.

'Remember your creator
    While music's daughters strut
With golden bowl and pitcher whole
    And silver cords uncut.'

Turn to the New Testament,
    Turn over with a thud,
'The sun will wear sackcloth of hair,
    The moon will turn to blood.'

The coal was six feet thick there,
    The roof a foot of Coombe,
With air ablaze, the ripping face
    Became a rock-sealed tomb.

Why won't it come to the surface?
    The winding engines stall.
After an age, they send the cage
    Back down to clear the fall.

The photographs in the vestry
    Start off in sepia;
Then every shade begins to fade
    And ends an empty square.

Each blackened name on a gravestone,
    Each cross inscribed 'I AM',
Breaks from its base, falls on its face,
    And worships the White Lamb.

For faces they will fail me,
    And names I will forget,
But music sung when I was young
    Is sound within me yet.

Time is an ever-rolling stream
    But shallow, streaked with weeds.
In spate or drought, this rock stands out,
    And, cleft for me, it bleeds.

# Suffolk Boy
*i.m. Chris Richardson*

Your stony grey beach is bleak and dull
as colliery slag-heaps or High Peak scree.
But the more you look the more you see
individuals, various, colourful.

Out of the rubble, a slow flowering
of lavender- lilac- heather-greys.
Jumble rewards the undaunted gaze,
attention being a sort of Spring,

another reminder that wonder works.
Just so, by watching, you learnt to swim,
and found the best kind of pebble to skim,
Coralline Crag and quartzite pucks,

so making a line through crests and plumes,
that even when sinking seemed the end,
the sea could reverse the verdict of land:
a stone that rises, a burden that blooms.

## Bramley Seedling

Stored winter apples'
breath on my face:
warmth in the cold.
A river unravels
to that orchard place
in the coalfield's fold,
to that brick box built
where the uprooted railway's
now a cinder track.
The years' black silt
was to bury me always
but I live. Take me back.

# Notes

'Pithead' – an invocation of the Muse. A 'snap-tin' is a lunchbox; 'snap' became slang for 'food'. 'Barkled' is a Nottinghamshire term for 'dirty'.

'Unlatched and Lit' – the title and the first line are from the poem 'Expectans Expectavi' by Charles Sorley, parts of which were set to music as a choral anthem by Charles Wood. It perhaps needs to be clarified that when a church is lit from within at night, stained-glass windows are dull and monochrome dark, and look like crocodile-skin on a handbag.

'Those Amiable Dwellings' – the title and the last verse of the third stanza refer to Psalm 84 in the version from the *Book of Common Prayer*. 'Brother James's Air' is a setting of the 23rd Psalm, popular with choirs in an arrangement by Gordon Jacobs. The end of the poem references Genesis 8:6-12 and John 12:24.

'Fauré' – the piece being performed by festival choir and orchestra is the 'Cantique de Jean Racine' by Gabriel Fauré. A line is taken from Racine's text – in English, 'Let all hell flee at the sound of your voice'.

'C90s' – the C90 was a 90-minute blank cassette with which you could make a mix-tape. The line 'I am at rest in you, I have come home' is, absurdly, from Dorothy L. Sayers' *Busman's Honeymoon* (1937).

'After The Death Of A Child (A Pastoral Heckle)' – the consolations referred to include the line 'And love is proved in the letting-go' from Cecil Day-Lewis' poem 'Walking Away', and the popular anthology of reflections on grief *All In The End Is Harvest*, edited by Agnes Whitaker.

'Baby Steps' – for 'man of calamity' see Jonah 1:7-8. A garbled reference is made at the end of the second stanza to the song 'Love and Marriage', as sung by Frank Sinatra.

'Aubade' – the poem engages with the original sense of 'Aubade' as a love-song for lovers separating at dawn.

29

'Toys' – when very young, my daughter occasionally 'borrowed' bouquets that were left behind after funerals and weddings in the nearby church.

'One More Last Word From the Cross' – Matt Carver was a brilliant student at Brasenose College, Oxford, who died of leukaemia in 2008, aged 22. I took the funeral in Newport Cathedral.

'Last of the Coalmine Choirboys' – supposedly, in the past, only choirs with royal approval wore red cassocks. The service of Evensong described has a hymn before the anthem; the lessons are Ecclesiastes 12 and Revelation 6. The last verse references the hymns 'O God Our Help In Ages Past' and 'Rock of Ages'.

'Suffolk Boy' – my father, remembered in this poem, grew up on the Suffolk coast, moved to Nottinghamshire to teach, and loved to walk in the Peak District.

'Bramley Seedling' – another poem set in Southwell, where the first Bramley Apple was grown.

# Acknowledgements

Thanks to all those who read and commented on these poems in manuscript: Liz Berry, Anthony (Vahni) Capildeo, Julia Copus, Matthew Francis, Kathryn Gray, Luke Kennard, Kay McCallum, Andrew Neilson, Jeremy Noel-Tod, Julius Purcell, Craig Raine – with particular thanks to Rory Waterman.